Unburdened:
A Single Mother's Journey to Freedom and Wholeness

Breaking Free from Toxicity to Reclaim Peace, Purpose, and Power

By

Cheli Gibson-Chappell

Published by

Huber Heights, OH 45424

copelandpublishingllc.com

Copyright © 2025 by Cheli Gibson-Chappell

All rights reserved.

No part of this publication may be reproduced, distributed, or transmitted in any form or by any means, including photocopying, recording, or other electronic or mechanical methods, without the prior written permission of the publisher, except in the case of brief quotations embodied in critical reviews and certain other noncommercial uses permitted by copyright law.

For permission requests, contact:

Copeland Publishing LLC

PO Box 24674 Huber Heights, OH 45424

Email: copelandpublishingllc@gmail.com

ISBN: 979-8-218-70822-1 (Print)

ISBN: 979-8-218-86736-3 (eBook)

Library of Congress Control Number: 2025921210

Front and Back Book Cover Design: Olu(@bmcdesign

Editor: Carol Dokes

Author photo by Expression Studios

Printed in the United States of America.

Table of Contents

Introduction
"Why I Chose to Walk Away."

Chapter 1: The Breaking Point
"I Can't Do This Anymore."..1

Chapter 2: Red Flags and Revelations
"It Wasn't Just One Thing, It Was Everything." 5

Chapter 3: The Decision
"Leaving Wasn't Easy, Staying Would've Destroyed Me."......... 11

Chapter 4: The Healing Plan
"I Didn't Just Want to Survive, I Wanted to Be Whole.".............. 17

Chapter 5: Rebuilding Me
"I Wasn't Starting Over, I Was Starting True." 23

Chapter 6: Becoming Her
"I Am the Women I Prayed to Become." 27

Chapter 7: A Letter to the Woman Who's Ready to Begin Again."
"Your Healing is not the End of Your Story, it's the Beginning of Your Freedom."………………………………...……33

Chapter 8: Spirit-Led Living
"Tapping Into Faith, Intuition, and Inner Peace, My New Compass"…... 37

Chapter 9: Rebuilding Without Settling

"Creating a New Life by Design, Not Default Relationship, Career, and Motherhood Included." 41

Chapter 10: Teaching Through Living

"How My Journey Has Shaped How I Parent, Love, and Show Up in the World." 49

Chapter 11: Teaching Healing & Wholeness

"Wholeness is the Legacy I Leave" 53

Chapter 12: The Woman in the Mirror

"Honoring the Woman I've Become" 57

Chapter 13: Unburdened and Unbothered

"Embracing the Freedom of Living Authentically and Unapologetically on My Terms." 61

Self-Help Journal- Part 1

Awareness 67

Self-Help Journal- Part 2

Reflection & Releasing 69

Self-Help Journal- Part 3

Rebuilding Boundaries 71

Self-Help Journal- Part 4

Moving Forward 73

Reflection Questions 75

Renewal Challenges 85

Acknowledgements..................................…..…95
About the Author.................................…..…97
Connect with the Author 99

Introduction

"Why I Chose to Walk Away."

There comes a moment in every woman's life when silence becomes too loud, pain becomes too familiar, and pretending becomes too heavy to carry.

For me, that moment wasn't a dramatic explosion. It was a quiet ache in my chest while washing dishes, folding laundry, smiling through meetings, and saying "I'm fine" when I wasn't. I had everything the world told me I should want, a husband, a job, a circle of family and friends, but I was drowning in the expectations of everyone but myself.

I was a wife and a mother, yes, but I was also a woman with dreams, emotions, exhaustion, and a voice I had long silenced for the comfort of others.

This memoir is not about blame. It's not a tell-all or a revenge story. It is not an attack on anyone's character. It's about *my* awakening and choosing to finally live, fully, freely, and on purpose. I wrote this memoir not just to share my story, but to give permission to every person who feels stuck in a version of life that no longer fits their soul.

Leaving wasn't easy. I had to walk away from toxic relationships, a job that drained me, family members who tried to manipulate me, and friends who weren't really friends at all. I didn't leave because I hated them, but because I finally loved myself.

Cheli Gibson-Chappell

This is a story of reclaiming my mind, body, and spirit, one boundary, one breath, one bold decision at a time. If you're reading this and you're in a dark place, or a place that just doesn't feel like *you* anymore, I want you to know that freedom is possible. Healing is possible. Wholeness is waiting but it starts with choosing yourself first.

This is how I chose me and why I chose to walk away from those relationships.

Welcome to my unburdening!

Chapter 1: The Breaking Point: "I Can't Do This Anymore."

I didn't scream it. I didn't say it aloud. I whispered it to myself in the quiet, as I sat on the edge of my bed in the early morning light, my children still sleeping, my husband in the other room, and my soul somewhere between numbness and rage.

It wasn't one big event that broke me. It was everything. It was the slow accumulation of being ignored, being dismissed, being labeled too emotional, too difficult, too much. It was waking up every day with a tightness in my chest and going to bed every night wondering if I'd ever feel peace again.

The marriage, the job, the people I called "family" all of it was draining me. Holding up the weight of a life that looked polished on the outside was silently crushing me within. I had mastered survival, but survival isn't the same as being alive. I was ready to choose more.

I told myself that I was just tired. That this was just a "rough season." That if I prayed harder, worked harder, loved harder, things would change. But deep down, I knew the truth: no amount of effort would fix what was fundamentally broken.

There was a night I'll never forget. After putting my children to bed. I walked into the bathroom, closed the door, and stared at myself in the mirror. The woman looking back at me was a stranger. My eyes were dulled. My spirit was weary. I wasn't just physically exhausted, I was also emotionally starved. I felt that no one saw me. Not really and I had forgotten how to see myself.

That was the moment. Quiet but absolute.

Not with drama. Not with chaos. Just a truth that stood up in me and refused to sit down again.

"I'm done."

Done pretending. Done shrinking. Done sacrificing my sanity to keep others comfortable.

In that moment, I chose to leave my marriage not just for me, but also for my children. I wanted them to see that sometimes; you must do what is best for your soul even if it disappoints others. I needed them to know that choosing yourself is not selfish; it is survival. It is strength.

I aspired for my children to grow up witnessing a version of me that wasn't just going through the motions. To see the best of me, the vibrant, whole, joyful woman I once was and could be again. I owed them that. But more than anything, I owed it to myself.

By the time I made the decision to walk away, my body had already begun to fight back. The stress and emotional toll had built up like a silent storm. I developed Bell's Palsy on one side of my face, a physical manifestation of the emotional paralysis that had long consumed me. My blood pressure spiked. I was diagnosed with Type 2 diabetes. My hair thinned. My weight plummeted from the mid-140s to 115 pounds. I was literally disappearing, and no one seemed to notice.

I noticed. My body was screaming what my heart had been whispering for years: "This life is killing me."

I didn't have a perfect plan, nor did I know what came next. I knew I couldn't keep sacrificing my health, my joy, and my sanity to keep up appearances. So I stopped. Because sometimes the pain that pushes you to your limit is also the force that sets you free.

That was my breaking point. It was the beginning of my breakthrough.

Chapter 1: Guided Reflections

When have you ignored your own needs to please others?

_____

_____

_____

What has your body or spirit been trying to tell you lately?

_____

_____

_____

Chapter 2: Red Flags and Revelations: "It Wasn't Just One Thing, It Was Everything."

People asked, "What happened?" But the truth is, by the time it was all falling apart, it had been broken for a long time.

I had gotten used to red flags. Learned to walk around them like furniture in a crowded room. I justified, minimized, and gaslit myself into believing things weren't that bad. But they were.

When I became a mother for the first time, I carried not only the weight of new life in my arms, but also the weight of expectations. Instead of leaning into responsibility, his father drifted away, leaving me to carry the role of both mother and father. When we separated, our son was just a toddler. I was a single mother for over a decade. When I decided to get married and had two more children, I believed I was giving my children the stability I'd always longed for. They would have a home with two parents under one roof. But the truth is, just because two adults live in the same house doesn't mean it's a healthy home.

After thirteen years, I had to face the painful truth that staying in a toxic marriage wasn't protecting my children.

It was slowly shaping for them a distorted view of love, sacrifice, and self-worth.

My marriage lasted longer than it should have not because I was weak, but because in my mind I was doing the right thing. I wanted it to work. I wanted my children to experience what I never had. I grew up with a single mother and had no relationship with my father, by his choice. That absence left a mark, and I didn't want that for my children.

Was I showing my best self? No, I was emotionally drained, physically breaking down and spiritually empty. What were they really learning from me? I wasn't modeling strength, I was modeling emotional depletion. I realized they deserved to see a mother who loved herself enough to leave. A mother who chose peace over performance. A mother who led by example, even when it was hard.

At work, the red flags resembled disrespect and became impossible to ignore. I was being treated and talked down to like I was a child. My input was disregarded, my every move was micromanaged, and the dedication I poured into my role was overlooked. I showed up early, stayed late, carried workloads that weren't mine, and still in those moments I felt small. With the experience I brought to the table, the way I was treated wasn't just unfair, it was demeaning and unacceptable. Then it clicked: I wasn't respected. The years of hard work weren't valued, and I was never truly seen. Just like in my marriage, I was being tolerated, not appreciated. And that wasn't enough. I thought if I just worked harder, stayed quieter, and smiled more, maybe I would finally be seen. I gave my best, believing excellence would speak for itself. What once felt like an opportunity began to feel like a cage. The constant pressure to prove my worth, the feeling of being overlooked and undervalued, it began to wear down my confidence and steal my peace.

It wasn't the work itself that wore me down, it was the people. I worked alongside employees whose negativity poisoned the atmosphere. Gossip, competition, and passive aggression became the norm. Instead of building each other up, some thrived on tearing others down. What made it harder was that management tolerated it. The very people who were supposed to lead with fairness, accountability, and respect chose silence or contributed to the toxicity. Their refusal to address the behavior or take accountability themselves spoke volumes. It taught me that in toxic environments, dysfunction isn't just allowed, it's often protected. Instead of asking how you can adapt to dysfunction, ask yourself: *What would it look like if I aligned with environments that celebrated me instead of tolerated me?* I tried my best to rise above it all. But the weight of constantly having to defend my worth in a place that should have recognized it slowly eroded my spirit. Eventually, I realized that no paycheck is worth your peace, and no title is worth your dignity.

That experience didn't break me. It built me. I made a promise to myself: never again would I hand over the power to define my purpose to an employer. I took my power back, fully and fiercely. I rebuilt what no one could ever steal from me: my confidence, my self-worth, and my God-given right to stand in my truth with unshakable self-respect.

Then there were the friendships, the ones I thought would be lifelong. I was always there for them, but they weren't always there for me. During their marriage crises, job meltdowns, family drama, you name it, I showed up. I answered late-night calls and listened for hours without judgment, I held their pain. But when it was my turn to break and fall apart they were gone. Where were my friends when I needed someone to just sit with me in silence or reassure me I wasn't crazy? My "so called" friends disappeared. That kind of abandonment cuts deep. But it taught me something powerful: I had to learn to give myself the love, the compassion, and the support I had so freely given to everyone else. I chose to become the friend to myself that I had always been to others.

All these red flags, and still I stayed. Because for so long, I didn't think I deserved better. I used to believe that being a good woman meant staying quiet, putting others first, and constantly sacrificing my own needs. Then the revelations came. Painful, but necessary.

I realized love without respect is just control. Peace isn't something you wait to find, it's something you fiercely protect. I reminded myself that I was not placed on this earth to continuously justify why I deserve to be treated with basic human dignity.

The more I listened to my inner voice, the one I had silenced for so long, the louder it became. And it didn't ask for permission. It demanded change!

The red flags I once stepped over became non-negotiables. The roles I once performed became masks I refused to wear. The relationships I once tolerated became reminders of what I would never accept again.

This chapter of my life wasn't about cutting people off just to be petty or out of bitterness. It was about breaking the chains that kept me bound to pain, performance, and pretending. It was about seeing clearly for the first time in a long time and choosing to walk toward freedom, even if I had to do it alone. Toxicity isn't always loud or obvious. Sometimes you don't see how toxic something is until you leave and begin to heal from it.

That is when my healing truly began!

Chapter 2: Guided Reflections

What beliefs about sacrifice have you carried from childhood?

_____

_____

_____

Where in your life have you stayed too long?

_____

_____

_____

Chapter 3: The Decision: "Leaving Wasn't Easy. Staying Would've Destroyed Me."

People like to romanticize the idea of walking away. They imagine a dramatic exit, bags packed, middle finger in the air, and Beyoncé blasting in the background. The truth is, making the decision to leave the life I knew, the life I had built around everyone else's expectations was one of the hardest, most gut-wrenching choices I've ever made.

It wasn't a single moment. It was a series of quiet confirmations. There were little signs from my body, my spirit, and even my children, all signaling that this version of life was no longer sustainable.

Emotionally, I had already started to disconnect. I was no longer begging for love or understanding from people who refused to give it. I stopped arguing. Stopped explaining myself and stopped trying to shrink my needs to fit into someone else's comfort zone. Emotionally leaving is one thing but physically walking away, that takes a different kind of strength.

The hardest part of leaving my marriage wasn't packing a bag or saying goodbye, it was seeing the fear and concern on my children's faces. The uncertainty in their eyes, the way they watched me, silently asking questions they didn't yet have words for. I had no answers at the time. I didn't even know what tomorrow would look like. But I did know one thing.

I couldn't fall apart.

"I have to be strong for them," I whispered to myself. Over and over, like a heartbeat. The weight of leaving hit me like a tidal wave so heavy I could barely breathe. It knocked me down in every possible way. Even in that moment, I knew deep in my soul, I would get back up.

Maybe it wouldn't happen right away or tomorrow, but eventually. It was just going to take time. The first few nights after we left, we stayed in a hotel. A few bags, with a few belongings. I had no real plan. I was a full-time student, unemployed and holding on by a thread. I tried to shield my children from the full depth of my fear while holding them close enough to feel safe. I felt like I had hit rock bottom.

But here's what I've learned about rock bottom: **God meets you there.**

In the midst of my uncertainty, God moved. He placed people in my path, angels in human form who reminded me that good still exists in this world. People who offered help without expecting anything in return. People who spoke life into me when I felt lifeless. They reminded me that even when I felt invisible, I wasn't. I didn't leave because I had all the answers. I left because I finally believed I deserved more than the questions that kept me up at night.

There's one day that will forever stay etched in my memory. I was sitting in my car at a red light, tears streaming down my face. My children were in school, and I had just spent the last of my money on the hotel. I felt like a failure.

Graduation was only two months away, and I was carrying twenty-three credit hours, nearly double a full-time load but I was determined to finish school. I had a 4.0 GPA, and yet, in that moment, none of it seemed to matter. I felt defeated, hopeless, and homeless.

I grabbed my cell phone and called my academic advisor, my voice cracked as I told her I was thinking about dropping out of school. The weight of it all, the financial stress, the emotional exhaustion, the pressure to hold everything together felt unbearable. I had nowhere to go, and giving up felt like the only option.

God had other plans.

About ten minutes after I ended that call, my phone rang. A woman introduced herself as a representative from student housing. I'll never forget her voice. It was calm, kind, and full of grace. She said she had heard about my situation, and because of my academic record, I qualified for a housing grant. There was a two-bedroom campus apartment available, and I could move in that day. My rent and utilities were covered as well as the use of the laundry facility until graduation. I picked up the keys an hour later.

That was nothing short of divine intervention. Just when I was ready to give up, when I felt unseen and forgotten, God stepped in. That moment reminded me that even when life feels like it's unraveling, He's still moving pieces behind the scenes. He doesn't always show up the way we expect, but He always shows up.

That day changed everything for me. It didn't erase the pain and disappointments, but it reignited my hope. From that moment on, I carried a new kind of courage with me, the kind that comes from knowing I am never truly alone, not even in my lowest moments.

After moving into our new apartment, I started creating a quiet plan, one step at a time. I stopped sharing my heart with people who had already shown they couldn't be trusted with it. I prayed for clarity, courage and confirmation.

I made a list.

What would healing look like? How could I still be present and whole for my children? How would I find myself again?

There were days I doubted myself. Nights I questioned everything. What kept me going was the vision, the glimpse of a future where I was free from toxicity. A future where I could breathe. A future where I could live again.

This decision wasn't just about leaving, it was about alignment. It was about choosing my future over my fear,

Unburdened: A Single Mother's Journey to Freedom and Wholeness

my voice over my silence, and my soul over survival. It was about choosing me, finally!

That choice changed everything!

Chapter 3: Guided Reflections

What did leaving something or someone behind teach you about your own strength?

_____

_____

_____

How do you define courage in your own life?

_____

_____

_____

Chapter 4: The Healing Plan: "I Didn't Just Want to Survive, I Wanted to Be Whole."

After the divorce, all the emotional chaos, and the dust finally began to settle. Nonetheless, I realized something simple but powerful, I was still standing, a little spiritual bruised and a little broken. That was enough to begin again.

Healing has its own rhythm, it bends, pauses, and rises, but always carries you forward. It doesn't come with instructions. What I knew for certain was this: I could never return to the woman I once was. She had poured herself so completely into everyone else that she had lost sight of her own needs, her own dreams, her own peace. Healing required me to release her. It called me to begin again not just rebuilding my life, but restoring my mind, strengthening my body, and nurturing my spirit. This wasn't about starting from nothing, it was about starting from truth.

Healing My Mind: Reclaiming My Thoughts

I needed to rewire my thinking. For too long, I had been conditioned to prioritize others, silence my pain, and to measure my worth through productivity and validation. My mind had become a battlefield, but I chose to fight for peace. Slowly, I began to reclaim it. I rewrote my truth.

Every day, I challenged the lies I had believed:

"You're a failure." → No, I'm brave for starting over.

"You're too emotional." → No, I feel deeply and that's strength.

"You're alone." → No, I'm learning to be present with myself.

Therapy became a lifeline. Journaling became a daily ritual. I wrote everything: my fears, my prayers, my dreams, and my disappointments. I stopped shaming myself for how I felt and started giving myself permission to feel it all. And little by little, the negative mental fog began to lift.

Healing My Body: Releasing the Stress I Carried

My body carried the scars of years spent just surviving. The stress, the silence, and the emotional weight had taken their toll manifesting as Bell's Palsy, high blood pressure, diabetes, hair loss, and sudden weight loss. But acknowledging that pain was the first step toward reclaiming my health, my strength, and my voice. My body had been screaming for rest and relaxation, and I was finally listening.

I started walking, sometimes just to clear my head, sometimes to cry. I began exercising, eating with more intention, and drinking water like it was medicine. I paid close attention to how my body responded around certain people, environments, and conversations. If something made me tense or anxious, I stepped back. I started treating my body like it was sacred. Because it is.

Healing My Spirit: Reconnecting with God and Myself

Spiritually, I was opened in a way I never expected and that's where healing and strength began to grow. I connected with God again. Not the version I was taught to fear, but the God who had carried me through it all. I talked to Him like a friend. I cried during prayers. I sat in silence and listened for the whisper of peace. It came not in thunder, but in stillness. Then when I thought I was catching my breath, my mother passed away unexpectedly. It shook us to the core. My children and I were devastated, enduring another emotional blow.

My mother was my confidant. My cheerleader during my divorce. She was the one person who knew the depth of my pain without me having to say a word. She encouraged me to stay in school, and I am forever grateful that she lived to see me graduate. That moment was priceless.

When my mother died, her absence wasn't just felt, it lived inside me. An ache that wrapped around my soul and held on tight. I knew I had to stay strong for my children, but I also knew I had to seek help. I couldn't help them through the grieving process by myself. The grief of losing her felt unbearable, a weight I wasn't sure I could carry.

I enrolled my children in counseling, not understanding how much I would benefit from it as well. Our counselor was an incredible woman named Emily. She was patient with me and my children, meeting each of us exactly where we were. Her honesty gave us clarity, her encouragement gave us courage, and her patience gave us room to heal. She truly understood us and helped us process our grief, trauma, and transformation. Slowly, she guided me in rediscovering parts of myself. Her influence was so profound, it inspired me to earn a master's degree in Clinical Mental Health Counseling. I wanted to be for others what she had been for us: a safe place, a light in the dark, and a reminder that healing is possible.

Losing my mother was the most painful experience of my life, but grief didn't stop there. What I didn't expect was the loss of people who were still alive. The family and friends I thought would be there for me were not. In their absence, I saw the truth, they were never vested in me, only in what I gave them.

This was the point in my healing journey when I had to be honest about certain relationships in my life, even the ones I never imagined I would have to reevaluate. Some of the most challenging dynamics weren't with strangers or distant acquaintances, but with friends and family whom I loved deeply.

It is difficult to admit when someone close to you consistently brings more harm than harmony. What I've come to understand is that love does not require you to tolerate mistreatment. You can care about someone and still decide not to allow their energy in your space. That's not cruelty, it's clarity.

I recognized that every time I explained myself to someone committed to misunderstanding me, I was exhausting energy I needed to heal. Every time I made room for someone who couldn't be happy for me, I was shrinking to stay connected. That's not the life I'm building anymore.

Now, I lead with grace and boundaries. I no longer try to convince anyone of my worth, prove my intentions, or seek validation from people who are unhappy with themselves. I don't wish them harm. I wish them healing. But I also wish myself peace, and that means making choices that align with where I'm going, not where I've been.

Sometimes the healthiest thing you can do is love someone from afar.

The Healing Plan Wasn't Perfect, But It Was Mine

There were days I wanted to give up, but I kept showing up. There were nights I cried until I fell asleep. I kept choosing myself. I kept healing not for a finish line, but for freedom. I just didn't want to survive anymore. I wanted to live, to feel, to thrive and to be whole. Slowly, I was becoming her, the woman I always knew I was, buried beneath the expectations, pain, and silence.

Chapter 4: Guided Reflections

What has grief taught you about your own strengths?

_____

_____

_____

In what ways have you learned to heal while still hurting?

_____

_____

_____

Chapter 5: Rebuilding Me
"I Wasn't Starting Over, I Was Starting True."

Starting over sounds like you've lost everything. But I hadn't lost everything, I had lost what no longer served me. What I was doing now wasn't about rebuilding what was. It was about building something new. Something true. Something aligned with who I was becoming, not who I had been conditioned to be. This time, I wasn't moving for survival. I was moving with intention.

Stepping Into Purpose

I started to feel a fire light up inside of me, slowly, then all at once. After years of silencing my dreams, I began to speak life into them again. Pursuing my master's in Clinical Mental Health Counseling wasn't just about a degree. It was a promise I made to myself. Writing this memoir was a promise as well. A vow that I would use my story to help others rise from their pain and losses.

My pain taught me empathy.

My loss taught me compassion.

My healing gave me clarity.

I wanted to guide people, especially women, through what I had walked through and to come out whole. That vision became my purpose. It gave me fuel. It gave me something to hold on to when the grief crept back in or when the "what ifs" tried to haunt me.

Setting Boundaries, Not Walls

There was a time when I didn't know I was allowed to have boundaries. I thought being kind meant being available. I thought being strong meant tolerating everything. And I thought love required self-abandonment.

As I stepped into this new season, I knew I needed boundaries, not because I was bitter or out of spite, but because I had learned how valuable my peace was. I no longer made space for people who only showed up when it was convenient for them. I no longer explained my decisions to people who never tried to understand what I was going through. I no longer let guilt guide my choices. Some called me selfish. Others disappeared when I stopped molding myself to fit their needs and I let them go. I realized that every time I chose someone else's comfort over my own peace, I betrayed myself.

I had friends try to guilt-trip me. Family members dismiss my needs. Employers disrespect my worth. Even people I loved try to shrink me with their expectations. But I no longer take that personally. That's not about me, it's about their discomfort with my growth. My boundaries aren't walls to keep people out; they're doors that stay open only for those who knock with respect.

If honoring myself makes someone uncomfortable, they never honored me to begin with.

I've learned that boundaries aren't just about saying "no." They're about saying "yes" to the life you deserve.

Boundaries became an act of love for myself and for my children. They watched me say no without apologizing. They watched me protect my time, my energy, and my heart. And I could see little by little, they were learning to do the same.

Self-Care: Pouring Back Into Me

A crucial part of rebuilding was learning to pour into myself without guilt and without apology. I booked massages, not just for my physical body, but for soul restoration. I laughed and danced at concerts, took myself out to eat, and found joy again.

One of the most meaningful changes was vacationing with my children. They weren't extravagant trips, they were sacred pauses that reminded me I was allowed to live and enjoy life. We created memories, reclaimed joy, and healed together.

I began to treasure my peace.

Reclaiming My Life and My Power

I began thriving. I was able to replace all the material things I lost from the divorce, not out of revenge or ego, but as a symbol of restoration. I was finally standing on my own two feet again and providing for my children's needs. It really wasn't about possessions. It was about proving to myself that I was capable of reclaiming my life and power. I created a life I loved waking up to. Every day, I was learning to love the woman I prayed to become.

Chapter 5: Guided Reflections

What does self-care look like for you today?

_____

_____

_____

How do you know when you're at peace with yourself?

_____

_____

_____

Chapter 6: Becoming Her:
"I Am the Woman I Prayed to Become."

There was a time when I didn't recognize myself. I was the woman with a heavy heart. A woman who carried everyone else's burdens, while silently losing pieces of myself.

But not anymore.

Now when I look into the mirror and see her. The woman I fought to become. The one who refused to let the pain swallow her. The one who finally chose herself when everything was telling her not to. The one who refused to settle for surviving. This woman is finally home within herself. This version of me is rooted, radiant, and real.

I Am Peaceful

I no longer wake up in fear or brace for the next emotional blow. I don't carry the weight of other people's opinions. Peace, for me, looks like quiet mornings with coffee in hand and laughter echoing through my home. My spirit is calm. It's no longer needing to explain my worth because I know it now. It's walking into a room and not shrinking to fit someone else's comfort. It's saying "no" and not explaining. It's resting without guilt. It's trusting God, even when I can't see the full path ahead. Peace is mine now and lives inside me.

And I protect it fiercely.

I Am Whole

For years, I equated constant giving with value. Now I know wholeness doesn't come from being perfect. It comes from being honest.

I've cried.

I've healed.

I've rebuilt.

Now, I'm no longer searching for love outside of myself.

I am love.

I am enough.

Just as I am.

I am her.

I am the mother who chose peace so her children would know what it looks like.

I am the student who didn't quit, even when the weight of life tried to crush her.

I am the woman who buried her mother and still rose in grace.

I am the friend I had longed for myself.

I am the example I wanted to see growing up.

I am her, the woman who walks in purpose now, no longer afraid of her own voice.

I am her, the healed version, the free version, the whole version.

I am her, the woman I prayed to become, and I thank God every day that I didn't give up before I met her.

Cheli Gibson-Chappell

The Image of a Woman

(A poem I wrote for my mother, daughter, and for me)

She is not defined by her age or wrinkles on her face

She's defined by the years she has fought in this human race

She desires to be treated with dignity, respect, and love

To be honored and treasured over and above

All the material things in this life

She's a daughter, a mother, and sometimes a wife

She's marched and fought for her place in this world

She's been an example for every little girl

She's served her country in wars afar

She's battled inequality and has the scars

She rises above the hurt and the pain

She is powerful, so you better know her name

If you peel back the layers of her wisdom and her mind

You will discover that she is smart, wonderful, and kind

History tells us don't underestimate the power in her hands

For this is the image of a woman and not of a man

I AM this woman!

Chapter 6: Guided Reflections

What parts of your past self do you honor and release?

_____

_____

_____

Who are you becoming and what excites you about her?

_____

_____

_____

Cheli Gibson-Chappell

Chapter 7: A Letter to the Woman Who's Ready to Begin Again: "Your Healing Is Not the End of Your Story, It's The Beginning of Your Freedom."

Dear Sister,

I know what it's like to cry in silence while the world expects you to smile.

I know the feeling of watching your life unravel while you're the only one trying to hold the threads together.

I know the ache of pretending you're okay, of showing up, serving others, pushing through, when inside you are running on empty: mentally, emotionally, and spiritually.

Let me be the first to tell you: **you don't have to pretend anymore.**

You don't have to sacrifice your peace to keep up appearances.

You don't have to stay where you are no longer growing, just because you're afraid to start over.

You don't have to be everything for everyone, especially when it's costing you, *you*. I know leaving is hard. I know healing is painful.

What's waiting for you on the other side of the
fear is something far more powerful, *freedom*. You deserve that.

You deserve rest.

You deserve joy.

You deserve to take up space.

You deserve to be seen, heard, and loved, not for what you do, but simply for who you are.

You deserve to become the version of yourself you dream about, not just a shadow trying to survive.

I was once where you are.

Full of questions. Drenched in doubt. Carrying the weight of grief and guilt.

Then something shifted. I chose me.

That one decision changed the direction of my life.

I didn't have a plan, I just had enough faith to take the next step, and then the next. Then the next.

Some days I cried through it.

Some nights I broke down.

But every time, I got back up. And you will too!

This journey is not about becoming someone new.

It's about remembering who you've always been underneath the pain, the pressure, the people-pleasing, and the past.

She's still in there.

She's strong.

She is waiting for you to choose her.

So if you're reading this memoir and wondering if it's too late to reclaim your peace, your joy, and your power, let me be clear: **It's not.**

Start where you are.

Cry if you must.

Pause if you need.

But promise yourself, you will not give up on *you*.

You're being **reborn**.

On the other side of this storm is a woman who is whole, healed, and wildly free.

She is you!

She is worth everything it takes to meet her.

With love,

From the woman who finally chose herself

Chapter 7: Guided Reflections

What does womanhood mean to you in this season of your life?

_____

_____

_____

How can you honor the women who came before you through your actions today?

_____

_____

_____

Chapter 8: Spirit-Led Living:
"Tapping Into Faith, Intuition, and Inner Peace, My New Compass."

I navigate my life guided by faith, intuition, and inner peace as my new compass. For most of my life, my choices were rooted in fear. Fear of disappointing others, and fear of being alone. Fear had a tight grip on me, shaping my identity, silencing my desires, and keeping me in places I had long outgrown.

Now I choose Spirit-led living!

It is no longer about pleasing others or measuring my worth by society's expectations. I trust the gentle whispers of God. I no longer look for approval, I look for alignment. It's the lens through which I see the world.

Faith First

Faith isn't just something I reach for in a crisis. It's the foundation I stand on daily. There were moments when I didn't know how I was going to make it, but I kept moving because I believed that God didn't bring me this far to abandon me.

When I was in the hotel room with my children, with nothing but uncertainty, faith carried me. When my mother passed and I felt like a piece of me was buried with her, faith cradled me. When I sat in counseling, peeling back layers I'd buried for years, faith steadied me.

God has shown up for me in ways I never imagined. He has shown me that His timing may not be mine, but His love is unwavering. He answered tear-stained prayers with divine provisions when I thought He wasn't listening at all. Sometimes people would ask me, "How are you doing it?" "How are you mothering, healing, rebuilding, and still standing tall?"

It is all God.

He ordered my steps and carried me when I couldn't walk. He answered questions in the quietest moments and sometimes, when I thought He wasn't listening at all. He sent angels just in time. Whether it was a kind word from a stranger, a financial blessing, or an unexpected open door, God was there all the time. His voice never left, even when I couldn't hear it clearly. When I finally got still, I heard Him say: *"It's time to tell your story."* This memoir is not just a reflection of my journey, it's an act of obedience. When God tells you to speak, it's not just about you, it's about who needs to hear it. It's about who your voice will set free.

Faith In Action

Living Spirit-led means faith is active. It prepares your heart, anchors your peace, and guides every step forward. Faith believes that what's meant for me will find me, but it also calls me to rise, to show up boldly, and to take the next step, even when the path is unclear. I may not always know what's waiting on the other side of the door, but I walk through it anyway, because I trust Who is walking with me.

There is undeniable strength in walking hand-in-hand with God, co-creating a life that radiates healing, purpose, and freedom.

Now, I walk by faith, not fear.

I speak with boldness, no apology.

Because I know deep in my soul that I am being led by something greater than fear. I am being led by divine purpose.

Creating Sacred Daily Practices

Each morning is devoted time with God rooted in stillness, steeped in gratitude, lifted in worship. In these quiet pauses, I draw His strength and remember His goodness. My healing deepens as I create holy practices that keep me grounded in faith and clarity.

I no longer rush into the day with chaos or urgency. I choose alignment. I choose to create space for reflection and rest. These pauses with God aren't luxuries, they are my lifeline. In these moments, I remember not just who I am, but Whose I am.

Healing is not the finish line I'm chasing, it is the way I live. Every day, I choose it. Every day, I walk in it.

Chapter 8: Guided Reflections

How do you recognize when you are living spirit-led mindset versus emotionally led mindset?

_____

_____

_____

What are ways you experience peace in your everyday life?

_____

_____

_____

Chapter 9: Rebuilding Without Settling:

"Creating a New Life by Design, Not Default: Relationships, Career, and Motherhood Included."

I didn't just want a new life, I wanted a better one. A life built with intention, courage, and care. After the storms passed, I had a choice to make: I could either live in the past, or I could rise with a new standard.

I chose to rise!

When God brings you through the fire, you don't go back to kindle sparks in the places He's already healed. Don't settle for halfway love, halfway peace, or halfway living. You can rebuild, step by step, truth by truth, and boundary by boundary. You could create a new life, not by default, but by design.

Relationships: I No Longer Chase What Doesn't Choose Me

One of the biggest lessons I learned was that love should not require you to lose yourself. I spent too much time trying to hold together relationships that were never meant to last. I've stopped chasing, begging, and proving myself. And you can too, because worth is something we carry, not something we earn. If a connection drains more than it fills, release it in peace. Romantic relationships are no longer based on chemistry alone. They must be rooted in mutual respect, emotional safety, and spiritual alignment.

Rebuilding meant more than just setting goals, it meant enforcing boundaries in every area of my life, including love. I realized that I couldn't move forward with the same patterns that broke me. That's when another lesson came disguised as a relationship.

A few years after my marriage ended, I entered a relationship with someone I genuinely thought would be different. He came into my life when I was vulnerable but hopeful, still healing but eager to experience love in a healthy way. At first, he said all the right things, showed up when I needed support, and gave the impression that he was emotionally present. I thought he was there for me. But as time passed, the mask slowly slipped. The emotional manipulation, the lack of accountability, the inconsistency, it all felt eerily familiar. That same toxic spirit I had left in my marriage had found its way back into my life in a different form.

It broke my heart to admit it, but I had to walk away.

This time, I didn't stay out of fear or hope that things would change. I disengaged because my healing and peace were too important to gamble with. This relationship wasn't just another disappointment, I felt it was a test. It was a mirrored version of my past, proof that I wasn't fully walking in my freedom. I was just repeating old patterns dressed in something new. But this time, I recognized the signs, listened to my inner voice, and chose to break the cycle before it broke me.

This pattern of behavior forced me to ask hard questions about myself. Why did I keep attracting emotionally unavailable or damaging people? What unresolved parts of me were still trying to earn love through sacrifice or silence? I realized that it wasn't just about them, it was about me too. What toxic behaviors was I portraying? When you have two people who are not whole, toxicity will find a place in the relationship. I had to change the way I saw myself and how I allowed people to treat me. I deserved more. Because I am more.

Walking away this time didn't feel like failure. It felt like alignment, and I had passed a spiritual checkpoint. I proved to myself that I had grown. That I had learned. That I would never again choose chaos over peace, or attention over respect.

I used to think I needed someone to complete me. I now understand that I had to become whole on my own so I could connect without clinging and love without losing who I am. Even with friends and family, I created new boundaries.

Silence That Spoke Volumes

There are few things more painful than the absence of someone who is still living, especially when that absence comes from family. When you're part of a small family, every relationship feels significant. There's no crowd to get lost in, and no buffer to absorb tension. It's just you and a handful of people who share your blood, your history, and, ideally, your heart. So when the distance grows, it isn't just space, it's a deep, aching void.

After my healing journey began, I noticed how certain family members began to drift. There was less engagement with me and my children. Then there was outright avoidance. It hurt deeply because in a small family, every absence is loud, and every silence is felt.

I once shared close bonds with certain family members. We had history, laughter, and seasons of support that I will always value. But as I began to step into a healthier version of myself, some of those dynamics shifted. My growth seemed to create distance instead of closeness. Conversations grew shorter, interactions more strained, and I realized not everyone could celebrate the changes I was making.

It wasn't easy to accept, but I came to understand this truth: sometimes your light feels like a challenge to those who haven't yet embraced their own.

I chose not to meet withdrawal with resentment. Instead, I met it with grace. I allowed space where space was needed, knowing that protecting my peace didn't mean abandoning love. It simply meant I no longer had to shrink to stay connected.

I learned that it was okay to outgrow people, even family. I stopped begging for closeness and started protecting my peace. Instead, I honored my growth and no longer minimized myself to protect someone else's stagnation. Family is supposed to be a place of refuge, not rivalry. And when it isn't, we have to redefine what family looks like. I've since built a chosen family, a tribe that lifts me, celebrates me, and speaks life into my purpose. They may not share my bloodline, but they honor my values, my faith, and my joy and I honor theirs in return.

Walking away from those old dynamics wasn't easy, but it had to be done. Silence has a way of revealing the truth, love is not always about clinging. Sometimes it's about releasing with peace, and setting boundaries that honor growth, healing, and freedom. My peace is non-negotiable. If someone can't honor the healed version of me, I no longer give them access into my new life. Though difficult, choosing peace over chaos may be the very act of courage you need to step fully into your freedom.

Career: I Work with Purpose, Not Just for a Paycheck

I walked away from a job where I did not feel valued and at first, it was terrifying. The security of a paycheck, the familiarity of routine, even the titles and responsibilities I had earned, all felt like anchors that weighed me down. I had to let go to find myself again. Choosing purpose over pressure was the change I needed to make.

Staying in an environment that drained me wasn't just a loss of time, it was a loss of joy, confidence, clarity, and vision. I had been shrinking myself to fit into a space that was never meant to hold my full potential. I had gifts, ideas, and a voice that were never truly seen or respected.

So I pivoted. I returned to college, not just to collect degrees, but to reclaim my sense of power. I poured myself into my education while managing motherhood, grief, and uncertainty. That wasn't just discipline, it was destiny in motion. Every paper I wrote, every late-night study session, every class I showed up to, even when life was falling apart was a seed I was planting in the soil of my purpose.

Today, I don't just work, I serve. I serve others with a passion because I know what it means to hurt in silence. I write because I know what it means to search for healing in the pages of a book. I speak because I remember what it felt like to finally hear the words, "You're not alone." I mentor because I've been the woman who needed guidance, encouragement, and someone to believe in her.

I work with intention. I work with integrity. Now I understand that fulfillment doesn't come from titles or paychecks, it comes from impact. It comes from being aligned with what you were created to do. It's not about chasing money but following my mission. Every door that opens now is a reflection of the choice I made to believe in myself first.

Now I show up every day to be that woman for my children and others.

Motherhood: Leading with Honesty, Strength and Grace

Being a single mother in the midst of my own healing journey was hard but it was also precious. I didn't pretend to be perfect.

My children saw me get back up. They saw me cry, pray, grow, and rise. I gave them something more powerful than the illusion of a perfect home. I gave them the example of a resilient, loving, self-aware mother.

We healed together.

We laughed again.

We rebuilt trust, safety, and joy.

I don't mother from guilt anymore.

I mother from wholeness.

That moment redefined how I live, love, and lead.

My Life Now: Designed, Not Defaulted

Nothing in my life is by accident or obligation. I don't say yes out of fear. Every space I enter must honor the woman I've become. This is the fruit of choosing myself. This is the reward of not settling. This is what freedom feels like.

You don't have to go back to what broke you just because it's familiar. You can build something new on your terms, with your values, and for your joy.

I did. I earned it.

Chapter 9: Guided Reflections

What does rebuilding look like for you right now?

_____

_____

_____

What values will serve as the foundation for the life you're creating next?

_____

_____

_____

Chapter 10: Teaching Through Living: "How My Journey Has Shaped How I Parent, Love, and Show Up in the World."

The beauty of surviving the fire is not just in the escape, but in returning to the ashes, stronger and ready to teach what once tried to destroy you. My life became a lesson, not just for me, but for those watching, especially my children. I came to understand that the most powerful teaching doesn't happen from a pulpit or a platform. It happens in the quiet, unseen choices we make. The hard decisions in the healing process.

For a long time, I believed parenting was about providing a stable home, discipline, and love. Those things are essential, but now I understand that what shapes our children most is not what we say, it's how we live. My decision to walk away from everything toxic wasn't just about reclaiming my life; it was about modeling strength, courage, and self-worth for my children. I didn't want them to inherit survival as their starting point. I wanted them to witness wholeness, boundaries, and joy in real time.

Every time I stood back up after being knocked down, I was teaching them resilience. When I acknowledged my pain but still chose healing, I was teaching them emotional honesty. When I stopped letting people treat me like I was disposable, I was teaching them self-respect. When I cried in front of them, prayed with them, and allowed us all to be vulnerable together, I was teaching them that strength and softness can coexist.

I love differently now. I love from a healed place, not a desperate one. I don't overextend myself trying to earn love. I don't stay where I'm not celebrated. I no longer stay where I'm only tolerated. That's what freedom taught me. Walking away from everything that broke me revealed: *I am enough as I am.* I want my children to internalize that truth for themselves and carry it into every room they enter.

Today, how I show up in the world is rooted in authenticity. I don't have time to pretend. I've endured enough pain to know that masks only suffocated the soul. I speak my truth not to be seen as strong but to remind others they are not alone. My story carries power, not just in the victories, but in the vulnerability. Teaching through living means letting others witness the wounds before the wins and honoring the scars that remain as proof of the healing. Healing myself meant healing generations. I broke generational cycles with tear-filled eyes and a heart full of hope. Now, when I look at my children, I don't just see the future. I see healing in motion. I see the reward of difficult decisions, every boundary drawn, and every prayer whispered in the dark. I'm not perfect. I now live with intentionality.

I've learned that is more than enough!

Chapter 10: Guided Reflections

When was the last time you truly saw and celebrated yourself?

_____

_____

_____

What lessons are you consciously passing on to your children or others around you?

_____

_____

_____

Chapter 11: Teaching Healing & Wholeness: "Wholeness is the legacy I leave."

As a single mother, I've come to realize that my healing was never just about me. It was about them, my children. Every choice I made, every step I took toward wholeness, became a silent lesson they were absorbing. Children don't just hear what you say, they witness how you live. And I wanted them to see a mother who was whole, not broken.

Breaking the Cycle

I refused to pass down cycles of silence, sacrifice, and survival. I wanted my children to understand that pain doesn't have to be permanent. That they didn't have to stay in environments that diminished them, relationships that disrespected them, or jobs that devalued them. I wanted them to know they had the right and the responsibility to choose themselves.

Conversations That Heal

I began having honest conversations with my children about emotions. We talked about sadness, anger, fear, and joy. I told them it's okay to cry, to rest, to ask for help. Healing doesn't make you weak; it makes you wise. Wholeness isn't perfection, it's honesty. I told them, "Never hide from your feelings; honor them. They are signals guiding you back to yourself."

Modeling Wholeness

Words weren't enough, I had to live it. They saw me set boundaries. They saw me say no without guilt. They saw me walk away from relationships that weren't healthy, and they saw me walk toward peace with courage. They watched me choose self-care as a necessity. They saw me pray, journal, and invest in my spirit. And in all of that, they learned that wholeness is not something you wait for, it's something you practice daily.

Planting Seeds for Their Future

What I hope they carry with them is this: Healing is possible. Wholeness is attainable. Freedom is worth the fight. If I could rise from pain and rebuild, so can they. And one day, when life tests them, I pray they'll remember their mother not just as a woman who survived but as one who thrived, and who showed them how to do the same.

Chapter 11: Guided Reflections

What cycles are you determined not to pass down to your children or loved ones?

_____

_____

_____

How can you model wholeness in your daily life so that others learn by your example?

_____

_____

_____

Chapter 12: The Woman in the Mirror
"Honoring the Woman I've Become"

There is something beautifully powerful about pausing, meeting your own gaze in the mirror, and truly recognizing the woman looking back. Not just her features but her fire, her faith, and her fierce resilience. I see her now. The woman I've become. The woman I've fought to be. She is not lost in the shadows of who she used to be. She is not silenced by fear, guilt, or the expectations of others. She is clear. She is grounded. She is free.

For years, I measured my worth by how well I could care for others, how much I could give, how much I could endure, how small I could make myself to keep others comfortable. I was everything to everyone but myself. But now, I live by a new truth: I am here to shine.

When I look in the mirror today, I don't see the woman who once cried in silence or questioned her strength. I see the survivor who transformed into a warrior. I see the mother who created safety and joy from the rubble. I see the student who pressed through doubt to rise with purpose. I see a woman reborn, not despite the fire, but because of it.

I don't seek permission to live boldly. I'm not waiting to be chosen. I choose myself every day. I speak with clarity, I move with purpose, and I stand in my power unapologetically. I honor my journey. I trust my voice. I walk in rooms knowing I belong.

I have learned that peace isn't passive, it's a choice. And healing isn't just a destination, it's a way of life. I forgive, but I don't forget who I've become. I love, but I don't lose myself in the process. I continue to grow, and I protect that growth with everything in me.

The woman in the mirror is not broken. She is bold. She is becoming. She is blooming in places she once withered. She leads with love, anchored in truth, and full of radiant joy.

This chapter of my life isn't about survival. It's about celebration. It's about building, thriving, and becoming everything I was created to be. I have no regrets. I look forward with hope. I no longer ask, "Why me?" I declare, "Why not me?" I am her. I am home and the best is still ahead. I now honor and protect the woman I have become.

And I will never abandon her again.

Chapter 12: Guided Reflections

How has your journey shaped how you love and connect with others?

_____

_____

_____

How do you hold yourself accountable to not going backwards?

_____

_____

_____

Cheli Gibson-Chappell

Chapter 13: Unburdened and Unbothered
"Embracing the Freedom of Living Authentically and Unapologetically on My Terms."

Living authentically means I don't apologize for who I am. It means I say what I mean and mean what I say, without second-guessing myself. It means I don't water myself down to make anyone else feel better. I've learned that people who love me, the real me, will respect my authenticity. Those who don't will fall away and I'm okay with that.

Unburdened by Expectations

I've laid down the weight of expectations that once felt like heavy chains: those from family, from society, from my job, and even from myself. I am unburdened now. I don't need to wear anyone's vision for my life like a badge. I am not defined by what others think I should be. I am the author of my own story.

Unbothered by Opinions

One of the most freeing things I've learned through my healing journey is that people will always have opinions. The world may whisper its opinions about me, but I don't listen anymore. I am tuned to a higher frequency, which is the voice of God and the truth of who I am. I don't need permission to live boldly. I don't need validation to know my worth. My confidence is rooted in divine purpose, and my steps are ordered by faith, not by fear. That's the power I walk in now.

Freedom in Boundaries

Living unburdened also means I've set clear boundaries, and I protect them passionately. Peace isn't just what I seek, it's what I require. My time is valuable. My energy is precious. No one is allowed to take up space in my life unless they add to it. I no longer make room for drama, negativity, or anything that threatens my peace and growth. I broke free from the chains that held me back, rewrote my story with courage, and rose into the freedom I was always meant to live.

Embracing Who I Am

I have made peace with my flaws and my imperfections. I am not striving to be the "perfect" mother, the "perfect" friend, or the "perfect" anything. I embrace the messy parts of myself. The parts that used to feel like weaknesses because those parts are what make me human. They are what make me real.

This Is My Life Now

I wake up every morning grateful for the gift of being myself with no excuses, no regrets. I walk through the world with confidence because I know who I am. I know I am enough, just as I am. I am unburdened from the past and unbothered by the judgments of others. I have broken free from the chains of toxicity, to reclaim peace, purpose, and power!

I am unbothered.

I am free.

I am unburdened.

Chapter 13: Guided Reflections

What dreams are you stepping into now?

_____

_____

_____

How are you breaking from toxicity and reclaiming your peace, purpose, and power?

_____

_____

_____

Self-Help Journal

"Healing From the Inside Out"
Part 1: Awareness

Goal: Recognize and Acknowledge Toxic Patterns.

Prompts:

Describe a relationship or situation that drains your energy.

_____

_____

_____

What are your emotional, physical, or mental signs of discomfort around this person or place?

_____

_____

_____

What boundaries have been crossed?

_____

_____

_____

Activities: Toxicity Tracker

Situation/Interaction	How did it make me feel?	My physical or emotional response.	What I wish I had said/done?
Example: Being dismissed in a meeting.	Invisible/Undervalued.	Tight chest, felt small.	Spoken up and asserted my ideas confidently.

Affirmations:

"I trust my inner voice. It's okay to walk away from what hurts me."

"I am no longer available for anything that costs me my peace."

Part 2: Reflection & Releasing

Goal: Understand the root causes and begin detaching.

Prompts:

What fears keep you tied to this toxic person/situation?

_____

_____

_____

Have you mistaken intensity for love or loyalty for obligation?

_____

_____

_____

What did you learn about yourself through this experience?

_____

_____

_____

Activities: Permission Slips

Write yourself personal permission slips, for example:

"I give myself permission to rest."

"I give myself permission to say no."

"I give myself permission to prioritize peace over people-pleasing."

Post these slips in visible spots, like your office, bathroom mirror, car, or refrigerator as gentle reminders that you have full permission to what's best for you!

Affirmations:

"I am no longer available for relationships that diminish my worth."

"I am enough as I am, right now."

Part 3: Rebuilding Boundaries

Goal: Learning to honor your needs, space, and intuition.

Prompts:

Who respects my boundaries? Who resists them?

_____

_____

_____

What energy do I no longer allow into my life?

_____

_____

_____

What boundary was hardest for me to set, and why?

_____

_____

_____

Activities: Healthy vs Unhealthy Boundaries

Situation/ Interaction	My Old Response	Healthy/Boundary Version
Example: Being guilted into plans.	Say yes and feel resentful.	"I won't be able to make it today, thanks for understanding.

Affirmations:

"My peace is sacred. I have the right to protect it."

"I am walking in truth, not fear."

Part 4: Moving Forward

Goal: Embrace new beginnings with clarity and confidence.

Prompts:

What version of myself am I becoming?

_____

_____

_____

What qualities do I now look for in friendships, partners, or workspaces?

_____

_____

_____

How will I celebrate my growth and boundaries going forward?

_____

_____

_____

Activities: Design a Vision Board Collage

Gather images, words, and affirmations that reflect your goals, values, and the life you're creating. Choose visuals that inspire personal growth, healing, and forward momentum. Let this collage serve as a daily reminder of who you are becoming and the dreams you are determined to bring to life.

Affirmations:

"I release what was. I choose what will be."

"I am proud of who I am becoming."

Journal Reflection Questions

Cheli Gibson-Chappell

Which chapters or moments in Cheli's story resonated with you the most and why?

Cheli Gibson-Chappell

What emotions did you experience while reading this memoir? Did any parts bring tears, anger, joy, or a sense of relief?

_____
_____
_____
_____
_____
_____
_____
_____
_____
_____
_____
_____
_____

In what ways did you see your own life reflected in Cheli's experiences?

_____
_____
_____
_____
_____
_____
_____
_____
_____
_____
_____
_____
_____
_____
_____
_____
_____
_____
_____
_____

Cheli Gibson-Chappell

How does Cheli's journey redefine what it means to be a strong woman or mother?

In your own words, what does it mean to live unburdened and free?

If you released every toxic influence, what would your life look like?

What would standing fully in your truth look like every day?

Unburdened: A Single Mother's Journey to Freedom and Wholeness

7-Day Renewal Challenge

Cheli Gibson-Chappell

Day 1- Write down what you're letting go of.

Day 2- Speak one truth out loud you've been holding in.

_____
_____
_____
_____
_____
_____
_____
_____
_____
_____
_____
_____
_____
_____
_____

Day 3- Do something kind today for yourself, without guilt. What will you do?

Day 4- *Set a boundary today and honor it.*

Day 5- Reflect on a moment when you were proud of yourself.

Day 6- Write a letter to your future self after your healing begins.

_____
_____
_____
_____
_____
_____
_____
_____
_____
_____
_____
_____
_____
_____
_____
_____
_____

Day 7- Make a joy list: 10 things that bring you joy and peace. Meditate on them.

Cheli Gibson-Chappell

Acknowledgments

First and foremost, I give all glory, honor, and praise to God. You have been my refuge, my strength, and my guide. Every step of this journey from the moments of deep despair to the triumphs of healing, was made possible because of Your grace. Thank You for never leaving me, even when I couldn't feel You. Thank You for ordering my steps, for lifting me when I was weary, and for speaking life into me when I felt voiceless. This memoir is a testament to Your faithfulness, and I will forever walk in the purpose You placed within me.

To my beautiful children, Ahmad, James III, and Desireé your unwavering love, patience, and support have been the anchor that held me steady through the storms. You are the reason I keep going, and I am endlessly proud to be your mother. Watching you grow has been my greatest joy and my deepest motivation.

To my late mother, Barbara J. Gibson, my confidant, my cheerleader, my eternal source of strength. You were my first example of resilience and grace. Your support gave me the courage to finish school, to heal, and to keep pushing forward when life tried to knock me down. This memoir is a reflection of your love and your legacy.

To Carol Dokes my steadfast prayer warrior, loyal friend, and now, my editor. Thank you for always reaching out, even when I didn't have the words to ask for help. Your unwavering love, faithful prayers, and gentle check-ins carried me through some of my darkest moments. Your encouragement to share my story came right on time. Editing this memoir with you by my side has been a true gift, and I will never forget the role you've played in my healing and growth.

To Emily H. thank you for being a vessel of God's grace during one of the most defining seasons of my life. From the moment we began working together, I knew your presence in my life wasn't by accident, it was alignment. I truly believe God sent you to us, not just as a counselor, but as a divine reminder that faith works through people.

To all the single mothers showing up every day and doing the best you can with the circumstances presented to you. You are seen, you are powerful, and you are not alone. From my healing heart to yours, this memoir is as much yours as it is mine.

And to every person who stood by me in the dark and celebrated with me in the light, thank you. You may never fully understand the impact of your presence, your kindness, and your prayers, but know that I carry them with me.

This memoir is not just my story, it's a tribute to the power of community, faith, and unconditional love.

With deepest gratitude,

Thank you.

About the Author

Cheli Gibson-Chappell is a native of California and a proud United States Air Force veteran. With a passion for leadership, mental wellness, and purpose-driven living, she has dedicated her life to empowering others through both her professional journey and personal testimony.

Cheli holds a Master's degree in Clinical Mental Health Counseling and a Bachelor's degree in Organizational Leadership. She is currently pursuing her Doctorate in Business Administration with a concentration in Leadership, continuing her commitment to education, growth, and meaningful impact.

She is the Founder and President of *Mothers and Daughters United, Inc.*, a 501(c)(3) nonprofit organization devoted to fostering healthy relationships, self-love, and emotional healing among women and children.

In addition, she is the owner of *Copeland Publishing LLC*, a company devoted to amplifying stories that heal and empower. Residing in Ohio, Cheli lives her life grounded in faith and the belief that true freedom comes from loving yourself, setting boundaries, and seeking joy and peace without apology.

She wrote this memoir to inspire single mothers and anyone struggling to break free from toxic relationships, offering hope that healing is possible and that it's never too late to rewrite your story.

Connect with the Author

Are you interested in bringing *"Unburdened: A Single Mother's Journey to Freedom and Wholeness"* to life in your space? Cheli is available for:

Speaking Engagements Perfect for:

Women's conferences

Church Groups

Mental health & counseling events

Veteran and military support groups

Single mother support programs

Book Club Opportunities

Hosting a book club? Cheli offers:

Live or virtual appearances (Q&A or discussion session)

Custom discussion guide & journal prompts

Bulk order discounts for 10+ books

Podcast or Media Interviews

Cheli is open to sharing her journey on podcasts and in articles, especially those focused on:

Women's empowerment, Motherhood, Self-Worth, and Veteran experiences.

Stay Connected Monthly

Get encouragement and inspiration from Cheli every month:

Monthly video reflections & short teaching affirmations

Journal prompts sent directly to your inbox

Join the community at:

🌐 www.copelandpublishingllc.com

✉ info@copelandpublishingllc.com

Unburdened: A Single Mother's Journey to Freedom and Wholeness